PARTICIPANT'S GUIDE

THE SECRET BATTLE OF IDEAS ABOUT

GOD

OVERCOMING THE
OUTBREAK OF FIVE
FATAL WORLDVIEWS

JEFF MYERS

transforming lives together

THE SECRET BATTLE OF IDEAS ABOUT GOD PARTICIPANT'S GUIDE
Published by David C Cook
4050 Lee Vance Drive
Colorado Springs, CO 80918 U.S.A.

David C Cook U.K., Kingsway Communications
Eastbourne, East Sussex BN23 6NT, England

The graphic circle C logo is a registered trademark of David C Cook.

The website addresses recommended throughout this book are offered as a
resource to you. These websites are not intended in any way to be or imply an
endorsement on the part of David C Cook, nor do we vouch for their content.

Unless otherwise noted, all Scripture quotations are taken from the ESV® Bible (The
Holy Bible, English Standard Version®), copyright © 2001 by Crossway, a publishing
ministry of Good News Publishers. Used by permission. All rights reserved. Scripture
quotations marked NLT are taken from the *Holy Bible*, New Living Translation,
copyright © 1996, 2007 by Tyndale House Foundation. Used by permission of
Tyndale House Publishers, Inc., Carol Stream, Illinois 60188. All rights reserved.

Paraphrased quotations from Mike Adams, Sean McDowell, Glenn Packiam,
and John Stonestreet are taken from interviews conducted by Summit
Ministries during the filming of *The Secret Battle of Ideas about God DVD*.

ISBN 978-1-4347-1153-3
eISBN 978-1-4347-1219-6

© 2017 Summit Ministries

The Team: Tim Peterson, Ron Lee, Amy Konyndyk, Nick Lee,
Cara Iverson, Jennifer Lonas, Abby DeBenedittis, Susan Murdock
Cover Design: Jon Middel
Cover Photo: Getty Images

Printed in the United States of America
First Edition 2017

1 2 3 4 5 6 7 8 9 10

051217

CONTENTS

THE SECRET BATTLE RAGES, AND YOU ARE THE TARGET

Life is about ideas. Ideas have consequences.

Dr. Jeff Myers

A battle of ideas is raging all around us, but we're often unaware of it. These warring ideas travel under different names and guises, often passing themselves off as something they're not. That's why they largely go unnoticed and are difficult for us to recognize. Yet ideas have an unmistakable impact on us. Many ideas are like toxic viruses stealthily infiltrating our minds and hearts without making their presence known. They fly under the radar, infecting our lives and inflicting damage that isn't immediately apparent.

We each have a way of thinking—a collection of ideas—that guides the choices we make and how we live. These ideas form our worldview. But how did each of us select these ideas and assemble them into a worldview? How do we distinguish between beneficial and destructive ideas? And most important, how can we develop a worldview that not only is true and healthy but also bows to the desires and authority of God?

Among all the ideas competing for our loyalty, which ones reflect what God wants for us and from us?

OUR APPROACH

The issues we'll discuss in this participant's guide are essential to an accurate understanding of God and his desires for the world. In each of the seven sessions that follow, we'll discuss what lies behind the ideas that seek to control us and our world. We'll also examine our commitments, priorities, values, and beliefs to determine the origins of these ideas. This process is critical because destructive ideas often disguise themselves as the best solutions to the most pressing human problems. These problems are universal and can be summarized in five core questions about life that most people ask at one time or another:

1. Am I loved?
2. Why do I hurt?
3. Does my life have meaning?
4. Why can't we just get along?
5. Is there any hope for the world?

Each of these questions reveals an important insight into our understanding of our heavenly Father and our relationships with him. The ideas we form to answer these five questions determine our worldview. A healthy worldview reflects good ideas, and an unhealthy worldview reflects destructive ideas.

For example, in the 1930s, few Germans would have supported Adolf Hitler if he had publicly announced that he intended to execute six million Jews. But when he appealed to German loyalty to the Fatherland in the wake of the devastation of World War I, he gained their unwavering support. (Keep in mind that Germany was considered a Christian nation when Hitler rose to power and unleashed his evil on the world.)

World War II put an end to Hitler's genocide, but what if the Allies hadn't shared an understanding that the Nazi agenda was evil?

Mike Adams explained that if cultural relativism is true, then there is no moral basis for freeing those in the Nazi concentration camps. Without an absolute standard, that liberation was simply the Allies imposing their cultural values on another culture.

Like the Nazi worldview, many worldviews today are based on bad ideas. But because these ideas masquerade as good ideas, we may be completely unaware of their destructive effects.

Written as a companion to the book *The Secret Battle of Ideas about God*, this participant's guide is designed to help you identify and resist the idea viruses that target you and offer false answers to the five major questions about life. The guide has been set up for group use so that participants can discuss what they're discovering about the origins of the most influential ideas in the world today and the power these ideas exercise over people and entire societies.

In session 1, we'll discuss how ideas shape our lives and worldviews. Sessions 2 through 6 focus on how five counterfeit worldviews (secularism, new spirituality, postmodernism, Marxism, and Islam) answer the five core questions people ask about life. These counterfeit worldviews advance the most destructive idea viruses in the world. Finally, session 7 presents a sixth worldview, Christianity, which is the only way of thinking and living that can satisfy our deepest longings.

Each of the six worldviews answers the five core questions in a different way. Which worldview is best? In the secret battle of ideas, the five counterfeit worldviews aggressively seek to convince us that their answers to life's questions are valid.

Examining each counterfeit worldview will enable us to more clearly identify and isolate the idea virus at its core and contrast it with the truth of the Christian worldview. Idea viruses continue to spread their deadly infection, but we can stop them in their tracks as we learn to recognize them, immunize ourselves against their influence, and seek instead to embrace the Christian worldview.

At Summit Ministries, when discussing topics—especially controversial ones—with people who embrace other worldviews, we employ a method of engagement that relies on honest inquiry. In each session, we'll use this method to give form to the discussion and guide us through the process of clarifying meanings, identifying the origins of ideas, examining the contexts of ideas, assessing truth versus falsehood, and considering the most likely outcomes of adopting false ideas rather than the truth. As we seek to engage people and transform culture, we ask the following questions:

- What do you mean?
- How did you arrive at that conclusion?
- Do you think that's the whole story?
- How do you know that what you believe is true?
- What happens if you're wrong?

As you begin this foray into the secret battle of ideas, keep in mind the following principles:

- Be who you are—no performing.
- Say what you think—you are not your ideas.
- It's okay to be lost or frustrated, but don't disengage.
- Love one another.

6-23-19

INVISIBLE WARFARE

The Hidden Forces That Shape Our Lives

**DISCUSSING CHAPTERS 1 AND 2 OF
*THE SECRET BATTLE OF IDEAS ABOUT GOD***

*Do not be conformed to this world, but be transformed by the
renewal of your mind, that by testing you may discern what is
the will of God, what is good and acceptable and perfect.*

Romans 12:2

You live in the crosshairs of a secret battle of ideas. The Enemy's
objective is to win this battle for your mind. Satan knows your life
will reflect the ideas you adopt. In fact, it's likely this battle has
already affected you, though you may not realize it.

Bad ideas are floating around us like infectious diseases. These ideas
sicken us and, worse, make us contagious. We can spread idea viruses
without even realizing that we ourselves have fallen victim to them.

We would never intentionally expose ourselves to a viral infection.
Yet when it comes to destructive ideas, it's as if we refuse a flu shot and
then invite crowds of people to gather round and sneeze on us.

We expose ourselves to idea viruses because these deeply flawed worldviews promise to deliver the things we desire, such as peace of mind or some form of spiritual power or protection against setbacks in life. Counterfeit worldviews mix a measure of truth in with the lies, making it difficult to identify the destruction that will inevitably follow.

At first a virus does its work without being noticed. It's only later, when we experience symptoms of infection, that we realize a virus has been active. This applies to our physical health as well as the ideas we adopt and live by.

The American system of government, for example, is known for upholding the principle of the rule of law. These foundational ideas, established in 1787, helped produce a strong, prosperous country known for stability and freedom. But not everyone embraces this way of thinking and living. In many parts of the world, the governing power changes as a result of a coup or revolution rather than through legally sanctioned elections. Much of the world's population lives under totalitarian systems, where only the ruler's decrees are binding.

Societies are organized around ideas, and ideas have consequences. Many of these ideas infect the minds of those who embrace them, such as the nineteen men from another part of the world who brutally attacked the United States on September 11, 2001, killing nearly three thousand people. After learning more about the ideas that inspire acts of radical Islamic terror, we can assume the 9/11 attackers were convinced they were doing the right thing. But in reality, they were following a deceptive worldview that justifies slaughter in the name of Allah.

Today, terror attacks continue with alarming regularity. A way of thinking that was previously unknown to most Americans now looms as one of the greatest threats to the safety and stability of the world.

REFLECT

What does the secret battle of ideas mean to you? I've said, "Life is about ideas. Ideas have consequences." What does this mean to you? Think about a time when you were influenced by an idea that had a distinct consequence, good or bad.

IDEA VIRUSES ARE NOT A RECENT DEVELOPMENT

The secret battle of ideas about God is not new. In ancient times, God told his people not to intermarry with the people from surrounding pagan nations because he knew the Gentiles would infect the Hebrews with false beliefs and lead them away from the one true God (see Deut. 7:3–4). Little has changed today. All around us are people who advance ideas that have the effect of blinding us to the way of God.

Two thousand years ago, Paul made clear in Ephesians 6:12 that "we do not wrestle against flesh and blood, but against the rulers, against the authorities, against the cosmic powers over this present darkness, against the spiritual forces of evil in the heavenly places." As we begin to identify the impact of the secret battle of ideas, we are faced with inescapable questions.

In chapter 1 of *The Secret Battle of Ideas about God* (pages 21–22, 24–27), I tell the story of Rick Rescorla, a military veteran and the chief of security for Morgan Stanley at the World Trade Center. Rescorla lived according to a handful of unwavering beliefs that led him to sacrifice his life for the people he saved in the south tower during the 9/11 terrorist attacks.

These words of Jesus fittingly describe people like Rick Rescorla: "Greater love has no one than this, that someone lay down his life for his friends" (John 15:13). Rescorla's commitment to saving lives, no matter the personal cost, stood in stark contrast to the ideas that motivated the actions of the terrorists that day.

REFLECT

How can we accurately recognize what is going on in the war of ideas? How can we tell the difference between an idea virus that leads to destruction and the solution a Christ-centered worldview provides?

WHICH WORLDVIEW INFLUENCES YOU?

The Secret Battle of Ideas about God looks at the five most widespread and influential idea viruses (see fuller discussion on pages 37–39 of the book). These counterfeit worldviews are as follows:

- **Secularism,** which claims that we can use human intelligence to control life and make it turn out the way we want.
- **Marxism,** which declares that life is about capital and that the true path to peace and equality is through violent overthrow of all existing social structures (government, economic systems, family, and religion).
- **Postmodernism,** which insists that objective (capital *T*) truth doesn't exist, only the subjective (lowercase *t*) truths we create for ourselves.
- **New spirituality,** which asserts that a higher consciousness or god force is at the core of reality.
- **Islam,** which teaches that everyone is born Muslim (in submission to Allah) and must conform to Islamic truth or be conquered through *jihad* (the struggle against anything opposed to Allah and Islam).

[handwritten margin notes: New Age, Star Wars, Opra Whimphry]

Each of these worldviews tells us something about God, right and wrong, life, the soul, society and government, law, money, and history. They often adopt disguises to keep their motives and strategies hidden. That's why they can powerfully influence people without their awareness.

We often hear that ideas are neutral, neither good nor bad but simply different ways of looking at something. This view treats ideas as if they're nothing more than topics for conversation. But in practice, ideas guide the way we live with thoughts and suggestions that purport to answer our deepest questions about life. The ideas we rely on to answer these questions reveal what we believe about God, and the answers we consider most valid shape our relationships with him.

A worldview is the collection of ideas that form our answers to these questions. Our worldviews monitor ideas we're exposed to and isolate any that appear destructive. But worldviews can also be porous, allowing destructive ideas to infiltrate our minds without our knowledge that it's happening.

REFLECT

Read Romans 12:2 and think about the steps Paul discussed for forming your worldview. How does this important teaching from Scripture apply to the secret battle of ideas?

We catch ideas from a variety of sources—church, culture, family, and friends. To live whole, satisfying lives, we need to catch good ideas and reject bad ones. This isn't as easy as it sounds, however. Everywhere we turn, it seems, we encounter ideas from our culture that combine to sway us in one direction or another.

Idea viruses bombard us daily and can multiply out of control. We find them on billboards, in Facebook posts, on television, in songs and movies, on the Internet, in the classroom, in relationships, and more. With so many ideas vying for our attention and loyalty, which ones do we trust?

The key to victory in this battle of ideas is developing a worldview that accurately identifies and isolates the bad ideas from the good ones. The thoughts we habitually chisel into the granite of daily life reinforce our worldviews and eventually become who we are. A healthy worldview based on Christ-centered ideas gives us something to live by and live for.

REFLECT

As discussed in the book, everyone is asking big questions about life. The battle of ideas rages around these questions. Identify the core life issue that is most pressing for you at the moment. Does your worldview give a satisfying answer to this question?

Rick Rescorla spent a lifetime cultivating the heroic ideas of standing strong and never leaving anyone behind. These ideas were so central to his worldview that he didn't hesitate when faced with sacrificing his life to save thousands on 9/11. Rescorla acted immediately to save as many people as he could because his worldview lay at the heart of who he was. In the end, he led nearly twenty-seven hundred employees to safety before he died.

GOOD IDEAS WILL WIN

Knowing how viruses work can prepare us to counter the attacks of bad ideas. We can't avoid asking the core questions about life that come with being human, and we'll always be driven to seek answers. But we need a reliable guide.

We can learn to trust what God has revealed about himself, the world, and humanity. Trusting his truth changes lives and ultimately the world. Ideas have consequences, and true ideas give life.

In chapter 1 of *The Secret Battle of Ideas about God* (page 29), I list five declarations of freedom based on a Christian worldview that help clarify a proper view *of* the world and *for* the world:

1. **I am loved.** Deep, unconditional love exists, and I can have it.
2. **My suffering will be overcome.** Hurt will not win. Indeed, it already has lost.
3. **I have an incredible calling**. My life has meaning. I bear God's image.

4. **I am meant for community.** I can overcome conflict and live at peace with those around me.

5. **There is hope for the world.** I am not doomed. What is right and just and true will win.

Bad ideas seek to convince us that love isn't real, suffering is meaningless, our lives have no purpose, we are alone, and despair is unavoidable. Only a strong, truth-based worldview can keep idea viruses at bay.

REFLECT

Choose one of the five declarations of freedom and reflect on what you believe personally about the statement. How does your personal belief differ from the declaration as stated? How do you know that what you believe is true?

STOPPING BAD IDEAS BEFORE THEY SPREAD OUT OF CONTROL

In chapter 2 of *The Secret Battle of Ideas about God* (page 34), I tell the story of critical-care physician Rob Fowler, who traveled to Guinea to offer his help during the Ebola outbreak in 2014. When he arrived at the hospital, he found that a rumor about doctors killing patients had frightened the sick away. Many Guineans died because of this rumor.

Thinking of bad ideas as viruses can help us see how ideas work. It can also help us stop bad ideas from attacking us and those we love.

Young people today are walking away from their faith in record numbers as they fall prey to the counterfeit worldviews of secularism, new spirituality, postmodernism, Marxism, and Islam. These worldviews make bold truth claims, but they fail to provide adequate answers to our deepest questions about love, healing, meaning, peace, and hope.

We need to become aware of these counterfeit ideas and arm ourselves to effectively combat them. Simply agreeing that these worldviews are false won't prepare us for battle. Once we're armed with truth, however, we can help others identify and fight off the idea viruses that have infected them. Let's look at a method—called the Four I's—that we can use to stop the spread of bad ideas:

1. **Identify symptoms of a bad idea.** Doctors can identify viruses by the symptoms they cause: aches and pains, fever, and so forth. Christians must be able to discern good ideas from idea viruses. A helpful tool is the Summit method of inquiry: What do you mean? How did you arrive at that conclusion? Do you think that's the

whole story? How do you know that what you believe is true? What happens if you're wrong?

2. **Isolate the bad from the good.** After identifying bad ideas, we have to look at how they spread so we can stop them. Bad ideas masquerade as something good—or at least harmless. Otherwise, they wouldn't spread. You probably wouldn't be tricked by an idea that explicitly promoted fear, disappointment, despair, or defeat. Because they give some truth but not the whole truth, bad ideas are like counterfeits. Counterfeit worldviews look and sound like the real thing. Their labels say they are genuine. But when you buy them, you don't get what you pay for.

3. **Inform others about bad ideas.** Don't only tell people the truth but also inform them about lies that stand against the truth. You give them a little of the disease so they can build an immunity to it. It's called inoculation. And inoculation worked against deadly viruses such as polio and smallpox.

4. **Invest in those controlled by bad ideas.** The final thing you can do to stop bad ideas is help people survive once they've been attacked. You can't "uninfect" them. But you can help them fight off idea viruses.

When helping others, remember that the truth must be administered with love and encouragement. We need to be sensitive to what each person can handle. Try to open up conversations by asking these questions:

- "Would you be willing to tell me what you're thinking?"
- "Have you considered ...?"
- "May I share something I've learned that has helped me a lot?"

REFLECT

How can we practically use the Four I's to protect ourselves against idea viruses? How can we use this method to help others resist the ideas that may influence them?

THE ONLY WORLDVIEW THAT CHANGES EVERYTHING

We combat idea viruses with the *only* antidote: the Christian world-view. This worldview says that life is about Jesus Christ, who was involved in creation at the very beginning (see John 1:1–3). The Creator God, the Lord of the universe, is a personal God who communicates with the people he created. The Word of God (Jesus) even chose to take on human flesh and live among us (see v. 14).

Jesus Christ is at the heart of Christianity. He has shown us not only who he is but also what he wants for us and from us. Other worldviews may offer interesting insights, but they ultimately leave us unfulfilled. Only in Jesus can we find answers to life's toughest questions. Unlike a sports league, the five counterfeit worldviews play by different rules and objectives. The Christian worldview, however, shows us the path to the good life. Jesus claimed to be *the* way, *the* truth, and *the* life (see John 14:6). He offers eternal salvation to anyone who trusts in him, but that isn't all. He doesn't just offer us a way to avoid eternal death; he also offers us a way to think as he thinks and feel what he feels. He shows us the way to truly *live*.

As we've seen, ideas have consequences. Adolf Hitler was convinced the Aryan race was superior to all others and that non-Aryans had to be executed. The nineteen terrorists who attacked the United States on 9/11 were convinced that jihad must be waged to bring infidels into submission to Allah. Wrong ideas often lead to death and destruction. Learning to catch good ideas, however, is the way to the good life we long for.

REFLECT

Think about the five declarations of freedom based on the Christian worldview. Do you believe in the Christian worldview and these declarations that serve as answers for the five major life questions? Think about some of the ways other worldviews answer the questions. Do you live with the secure understanding of these declarations of freedom? If not, which ones do you question?

6-30-19
God is Love? + personal!
John 17
Zep. 3:17

AM I LOVED?

How Idea Viruses Make Us Feel Unappreciated,
Unwanted, and Alone

DISCUSSING CHAPTERS 3 AND 4 OF
THE SECRET BATTLE OF IDEAS ABOUT GOD

The LORD ... will rejoice over you with gladness; he will quiet
you by his love; he will exult over you with loud singing.

Zephaniah 3:17

There is a question you can't help but ask. It's unavoidable because it goes hand in hand with being human. Although the question is universal, searching for the answer can—and often does—lead us in wrong directions.

Each of us wants to know whether we are loved. The multitude of false answers to the question "Am I loved?" clamor for our attention and devotion. Widespread and highly influential idea viruses have distorted the search for love, including Darwinism, which reduces love to physical impulses, and the sexual revolution, which separates sex from love and commitment.

According to author and speaker Sean McDowell, the problem with the sexual revolution wasn't that people were looking for love but that they were looking for it in the wrong places. The idea virus of the sexual revolution has resulted in unnecessary heartbreak, or worse, for those who have fallen for it. But people who know God also know that love far surpasses mere physical impulses.

As humans, we want to know we're loved, and that makes us vulnerable to destructive worldviews. The desperate search for love can literally place us in life-threatening situations. It has even driven some people into the arms of radical Islamic terrorists, who are looking for weaknesses to exploit.

The five core questions that everyone asks at one time or another aren't merely interesting topics to ponder; they are longings of the heart that move us to seek answers.

REFLECT

Think back over the past several years and identify an event or a series of events in your life that was spurred by a search for love. Recall where that search led you. As you reflect on this, do you see counterfeit worldviews about love revealed?

WHEN THE SEARCH FOR LOVE TURNS DANGEROUS

In chapter 3 of *The Secret Battle of Ideas about God* (pages 45–47), I tell the story of Alex, a lonely woman who was drawn into an online relationship with an ISIS recruiter. Taking advantage of her vulnerability, the recruiter (Faisal) showered her with attention and gifts, promising that ISIS would satisfy her longing for love and a place to belong. Desperate to end her loneliness, Alex opened herself to a lie.

We are more like Alex than we may realize. God designed us to give and receive love, yet many of us feel deprived of true love. Each of us is vulnerable to idea viruses that promise love and acceptance. For some, the virus is deadly. Many are tempted to settle for less than the best, even allowing mistreatment or abuse just to satisfy their love hunger. Sadly, their quest leads them in the wrong direction, leaving them worse off than before.

REFLECT

Read and reflect on 1 Peter 5:7; Zephaniah 3:17; Romans 8:38–39; and Hebrews 13:5. Based on these passages, what are God's attitude and actions toward you? When you say, "I am loved," what do you mean?

unconditional Love

Trusting in God

HOW BAD IDEAS EXPLOIT OUR LONGING FOR LOVE

The abundance of broken relationships shows that false paths to love have lost none of their appeal. If we want to find true love, we must identify the counterfeits and isolate the worldviews that make us particularly vulnerable to exploitation. These are necessary first steps because counterfeits don't announce themselves for what they really are.

We seek authentic love, not a lie designed to destroy us. Why, then, is it so difficult to understand that we're already loved simply for who we are? Why do so many of us end up in relationships that prove to be the opposite of what we desire most?

Counterfeit worldviews present just enough truth to get people to believe a bigger lie. This is particularly true of the secular worldview regarding love. This idea virus has gained the upper hand in much of our society, especially in the way most people approach love, intimacy, and sex.

The secular worldview would have us believe that nothing outside the material world exists. The Enlightenment gave birth to this viewpoint and eventually led to the Darwinian evolutionary views. According to Darwin, humans are just complex animals, so suggesting that we should restrain our sexual urges is unnatural. Like Darwin, Sigmund Freud and Alfred Kinsey held the view that love is merely a natural physiological response to sexual stimuli.

Secularists argue that since the material world is all that exists, there is no right or wrong way to express sexual desire. Sex is about the survival of the species through procreation, and nothing more. Saying "I love you," therefore, is only an expression of hormonal reactions or a protective instinct to enhance the chances of survival.

Ultimately, secularism fumbles when it comes to explaining why people love, *don't* love, or even hate one another.

In chapter 3 of *The Secret Battle of Ideas about God* (pages 53–54), I paint a personal picture of the effects of the secular worldview I was exposed to in college. Believing the secularist lie about love, I indulged my sexual impulses. But ideas have consequences, and the consequences I suffered went much deeper than getting my girlfriend pregnant, paying for an abortion, and breaking up. The biggest casualty of this secularist idea virus was a healthy view of relational intimacy. Fear of getting close to anyone emotionally caused me to alternate between intimacy and isolation.

Given the prevalence of sexual activity in our society today, especially among high school and college students, humanity should be feeling incredibly loved. But disconnecting the act of sex from lifelong commitment has created a national health nightmare of sexually transmitted diseases (STDs).

In fact, pursuing intimacy through premarital sexual transactions defeats the very thing most people say they seek: authentic love. Instead, it can lead to a host of emotional and relational problems. The epidemic of pornography has caused even more damage.

Ideas are not neutral; they lead to action. They inspire and motivate. Anyone who has accepted and acted on the most common lies about love knows this.

REFLECT

Think of a time you experienced or observed the far-reaching consequences of a loved one's or friend's belief in a worldly, counterfeit lie about
love. How did the counterfeit love lure the person in, and what were the
most damaging outcomes? In retrospect, what could your friend have done
to protect him- or herself from the idea virus of counterfeit love?

THE BIBLE'S TRUTH ABOUT LOVE

Scripture tells us that Jesus *really does* meet our hearts' deepest
longings. In the Gospels, we read his teachings and the example
he set. So what does living according to Jesus's definition of *love*
look like?

In chapter 4 of *The Secret Battle of Ideas about God* (pages 59–61),
I share the story of Linda White, whose daughter was raped and shot
multiple times when she stopped to help two teenage boys with their
disabled car.

Understandably, Linda was overcome with grief and anger after
losing her daughter in such a brutal way. But somehow her grief
was transformed into a kind of love that counterfeit worldviews fail
to explain. Linda forgave her daughter's killers and, in the process,
brought hope to thousands.

Rather than giving in to hate, Linda chose to love her daughter's killers and even met with one of them (Gary Brown). Love not only changed Linda, who became an advocate of restorative justice, but it also transformed the life of Gary Brown. A Christian worldview transforms love itself, bringing good into the world even in the midst of personal loss.

The apostle Paul is another example of the transforming power of love. Once a sworn enemy of Jesus and his followers, he encountered love (the risen Christ) on the road to Damascus and became the greatest missionary and church planter of the ancient world (see Acts 26:12–18).

The secularist idea of love destroys lives, but God's love transforms everyone and everything it touches.

REFLECT

Read Luke 6:27–30 and Matthew 6:14–15, and think about the story of Linda White and her daughter's murderer, Gary Brown. How do you think you might react to the idea of forgiving the person who took the life of someone so precious to you? What is the power of love and forgiveness, and how can it transform tragedy into something positive for both parties?

THE NEXT STEP

As the secret battle of ideas rages, the Christian worldview reveals a deep, radically different love from the everyday kind we refer to when we talk about food, TV shows, and pets. We can take refuge in this love because it's based on two pillars of truth: God is personal (not an impersonal force), and he is present. (See page 62 in the book for more details.)

When Jesus came to earth, he showed us God's selfless, self-giving *agape* love, and that love changed the world forever. Agape love also changes people. When Linda White forgave Gary Brown, it transformed his life as well as Linda's.

In 1 Corinthians 13, the apostle Paul described what agape love looks like: "Love is patient and kind; love does not envy or boast; it is not arrogant or rude.... Love bears all things, believes all things, hopes all things, endures all things" (vv. 4–5, 7). Agape comes from God, and he is the one who pours it into our hearts by his Holy Spirit (see Rom. 5:5).

Agape is highly appealing as an idea, but committing to a life of selfless love seems daunting. We can easily feel that the bar is set too high, that too much is expected of imperfect humans. On the other hand, isn't selfless love what we want from others? Agape doesn't require us to perform or look a certain way to earn acceptance. There is no perfect standard to measure up to. God's love for us is unconditional, based not on our performance but on Christ's sacrifice on our behalf.

The secular worldview tries to force its counterfeit idea of love on us. But God's love strengthens our hearts and empowers us to resist the idea viruses that make us feel unloved and unloving.

REFLECT

Read John 3:16; Acts 20:35; 1 Corinthians 13:4–7; 1 John 3:16–17; and 4:7–21. What are some practical aspects of agape? How can anyone know that agape love is truly the only pure—and most desired—form of love?

Actions speak louder than words?
Have a forgiving spirit?

SELFLESS LOVE STOPS IDEA VIRUSES

Instead of heaping condemnation on her daughter's murderers, Linda White allowed her grief to spur her on to love and forgive them. This is what we're instructed to do in Luke 6:27–28. It's impossible to explain in purely human terms why we would ever forgive those who harm us. But in stark contrast to counterfeit worldviews like secularism that drive us away from love, the Christian worldview moves us closer to it.

You want to know where love is? He's right here. Eating. Drinking. Weeping. Conversing. Healing. God became flesh and lived among us (see John 1:14). Jesus is proof that God is personal and present. Other gods rule through instilling fear and taking life. Jesus gave his life for us and overcame fear.

Selfless love enriches our lives in three ways. First, selfless love enriches our lives by meeting our need for intimacy. In chapter 4 of *The Secret Battle of Ideas about God* (pages 65–67), I talk about a marriage-counseling session in which the therapist asked me to list my top five emotional needs. After writing down the first four (*Respect, Sense of purpose, Peace,* and *Feeling needed*), I added *Intimacy* to the list and commented that God couldn't possibly meet this need. After all, I would never experience sexual intimacy with him.

But after looking up Bible verses that answered the question "How can God meet my deepest needs for intimacy?" I realized that God cares for me, he rejoices over me with singing, he will never leave me, and nothing can separate me from his love (see 1 Pet. 5:7; Zeph. 3:17; Heb. 13:5; Rom. 8:38–39).

When life spins out of control, God is the only one who can meet our deepest needs for intimacy.

Second, selfless love enriches our lives by growing through giving rather than getting. We all long for God and his love, but idea viruses have convinced us that getting is the source of authentic love, not giving.

Unlike secularism, in which people substitute sex for religion to meet deeper needs, the Christian worldview says we're more blessed when we give than when we receive (see Acts 20:35). Love isn't a means to an end; it *is* the end, as Jesus demonstrated.

Selfless love changes the hearts of those who give it as well as those who receive it. It also changes how we live on a very practical level. People who give tend to have a greater sense of purpose and meaning than those who focus on getting. And this sense of purpose often leads to a longer, richer life.

Finally, selfless love enriches our lives by taming self-love. Unlike counterfeit worldviews, the Christian worldview offers the only plausible explanation for reaching out to our enemies, as Linda White did. Jesus said, "Love your enemies, do good to those who hate you, bless those who curse you, pray for those who abuse you" (Luke 6:27–28). The love of Jesus transforms us, enabling us to love our enemies.

But our culture worships self-love. Marketers tell us we "deserve" what they're selling. Narcissists demand that we advance their interests at our own expense, and they become angry when they don't get their way.

Even King David showed narcissistic tendencies. Though he was a man after God's own heart (see 1 Sam. 13:14), he fell for the idea virus of self-love, seducing a loyal friend's wife and then orchestrating his friend's death. But when David repented of his sin, asking God to give him a clean heart and a right spirit (see Ps. 51:10), he left his narcissism behind. From that point on, he lived to please God instead of himself. Like David, we were made to be lovers. But self-love leads to destruction. Only as we dwell in God's selfless love can self-love be tamed and transformed.

REMEMBER THE FOUR I'S WHEN COMBATING BAD IDEAS ABOUT LOVE

1. Identify symptoms of a bad idea.
2. Isolate the bad from the good.
3. Inform others about bad ideas.
4. Invest in those controlled by bad ideas.

WHAT DOES ALL THIS MEAN?

The Creator of the universe meets our deepest needs for intimacy through his love. With those needs met, we're free to live in a radically different way. This sets the Christian worldview apart from counterfeit worldviews. In chapter 4 of *The Secret Battle of Ideas about God* (pages 70–72), I list five steps you can take to experience authentic love:

1. **Experience forgiveness and offer it.** Ask Jesus to forgive you and then offer forgiveness to others.

2. **Let God take care of the timing.** Instead of falling victim to an idea virus about love and sex, remember that only God can meet your deepest needs for intimacy. Accept his unconditional love and then focus on giving love instead of getting it.

3. **Don't just give to others what they want from you.** Selfless love does what is *right* for others, which isn't always what they want. This interrupts their obsession with getting, just as Christ interrupts ours. Reach out to someone with this kind of love.

4. **Be chaste.** Chastity means saying yes to sex within the boundaries of God's design. Biblical standards for chastity may seem strict, but they eliminate confusion and enhance true intimacy. God intends for us to treat others like persons, not objects. Do you need to make changes in your sexual standards and behavior to reflect God's standards?

5. Stay focused on God's perspective. Instead of falling for counterfeit ideas about love, ask God to show you how he sees it. In his eyes, giving is receiving. Selfless love reflects the love God has for you. Look for ways to give to others without expecting to be repaid.

When we grasp the depth of God's love for us, our love for others is awakened. Linda White's story shows us the practical side of selfless love. This kind of love rescues us from idea viruses that make us feel lonely and inadequate.

We're free to follow a path of self-love that focuses on fulfilling our own desires, or we can pursue God's way of love that gives selflessly to others. On the surface, the secular worldview seems far more appealing to our human nature. The choice is ours, but what happens if we choose the wrong path?

REFLECT

Select one of the five steps for experiencing authentic love. What are some practical things you can do to put this step into action during the coming week? Consider what struggles you may have, and take time to pray about them now and through the week. Later on in the week, try to come back to this question to reflect on what changes this action is bringing about in your life.

Pantheism - many Gods
oneness ⤵ all is God & God is all

Hinduism brought to USA by "Beetles"
⤵ Atman is Brahman
Human soul   Devine soul

Reborn   Born   Samsara   Maya is
                                 the illusion
                                 of this live.
              Live   Karma
    die   ↓
                     cause + effect

Romans 1 + 2

SESSION 3

WHY DO I HURT?

How Idea Viruses Fail Us in Our Suffering

DISCUSSING CHAPTERS 5 AND 6 OF
THE SECRET BATTLE OF IDEAS ABOUT GOD

This light momentary affliction is preparing for us an
eternal weight of glory beyond all comparison.

2 Corinthians 4:17

Life comes with pain and suffering. We grieve the loss of people we love. We might face chronic illness, the loss of a job or a valued relationship, or other circumstances that disrupt our lives and leave us wondering why this happened to us. We know the pain of being lied to and about, especially when the person spreading untruths is someone we thought was trustworthy.

We feel powerless to stop the bad things that happen. This might explain the fascination with superheroes in popular culture today. We wish someone would just swoop in and fix things. But instead we encounter one setback after another, with seemingly no one around to help.

If we could somehow make everything right, we'd do it. But that's not how things are. We don't have to look far to find a reason to ask, "If God loves us, why does he allow all this pain and suffering?"

With so much suffering in life, there is no shortage of idea viruses that promise to solve the problem. In this session, we'll look at the worldview of new spirituality, which views pain and suffering as an illusion. Seriously, an illusion? Anyone who has faced intense pain—physical, emotional, or otherwise—knows that pain is real. So why are so many people exploring new spirituality?

John Stonestreet, president of the Colson Center for Christian Worldview, asks why suffering hurts so much if it's only an illusion. Referring to the glib response of new spiritualists following the 9/11 terrorist attacks, Stonestreet argues that it's easy to tell people to keep a positive focus when you're not the one who is suffering. A non-answer like this is merely a way to avoid pain. If you're in deep pain, a nonanswer is almost worse than no answer at all.

Glenn Packiam, a pastor and the author of *Discover the Mystery of Faith*, reminds us that two-thirds of the Psalms are laments. He notes that we don't take our complaints to those who either don't care or can't do anything about them. Instead, we take them right to the top: to God.

However, if God is all-powerful and all-loving, why does he allow all this pain, violence, and destruction? And as we consider the false promises of idea viruses, does new spirituality offer anything at all that might help?

Loss and unjust treatment are matters that can't easily be overlooked. They often seem to come out of nowhere, creating chaos and undeserved suffering.

REFLECT

Recall a time of loss or another type of pain that seemed as if it would never end. Where did you look for help? What were the most beneficial resources you found, as well as any unexpected sources of help? What did you try that turned out *not* to be helpful?

IT'S POSSIBLE TO IGNORE PAIN—UNTIL IT HITS HOME

Most of us get caught up in daily responsibilities and give little thought to other matters. Then something happens to disrupt the familiar routine, making it impossible to overlook the personal reality of suffering.

C. S. Lewis wrote that "pain insists upon being attended to. God whispers to us in our pleasures, speaks in our conscience, but shouts in our pain: it is His megaphone to rouse a deaf world."[1]

In chapter 5 of *The Secret Battle of Ideas about God* (pages 73–74), I write about the pain of a failing marriage. I begged God to heal my marriage and take away my suffering. I had heard about God taking away other people's difficulties, but I just couldn't see my situation ever improving.

Disease. Betrayal. Loss. Regret. There is no way to escape pain. As we wonder why we have to endure so much suffering, it's almost a given that the next question will be "Where is God in this?" When we experience severe pain, we can't deny that a gap exists between reality and how things ought to be (or the way we'd prefer them to be). It's not surprising that many people blame God for this state of affairs.

Pain calls into question everything we thought we knew was true. The counterfeit worldview of new spirituality tries to explain why we hurt and what we should do about it. But does this worldview help us live better lives or merely deepen our despair?

REFLECT

Read Jeremiah 12:1; Psalm 13:1–2; Luke 22:42; Job 2:4–10; John 16:3; and Romans 8:18. Think about your most recent encounter with personal suffering. What brought it on? What was your honest thinking about God as you dealt with suffering? What was the outcome?

IS PAIN MEANINGLESS?

Many people, like Holocaust survivor Viktor Frankl, have discovered that when suffering has meaning, they can often find a way to bear up under the pain. But if suffering seems meaningless, pain and despair are magnified.

When I broke my neck in a car accident in college, I found meaning in the pain because God used it to set me on a new path that brought me back to him. (Read the full story in the book on pages 76–77.) I still hurt from that injury, but the pain is not meaningless.

The apostle Paul boasted about his weaknesses because they revealed God's power (see 2 Cor. 11:30; 12:7–10). As he observed, our weaknesses give us more reason to trust God, not less.

Read Romans 8:28, and think of pain or suffering that seems meaningless, cruel, or undeserved. What separates meaningful suffering from pain that has no meaning?

all things work together for good!

WHAT CAUSES SUFFERING, AND HOW DO WE STOP IT?

Why do you think there is so much pain and suffering in the world? Where is God in our suffering? As we struggle with suffering, we can't avoid asking yet another question: How do we stop the hurt? We tend to think that if we can figure out the cause of our pain, we can find a way to end it. This assumption is closely linked to our struggle with why a loving God allows pain and suffering in the first place.

Many people have said to me, "I could never believe in a God who would allow people to suffer." The dilemma of suffering isn't a simple one that can be addressed with a quick platitude. The Christian worldview alone offers a plausible response: we must focus squarely on the presence of evil and the brokenness it causes. Other worldviews struggle to explain evil and suffering.

Of the five counterfeit worldviews, new spirituality is the one that most seriously considers the emotional side of the problem of pain. Four of the false worldviews blame suffering on external causes—nature (secularism), the wealthy class (Marxism), culture (postmodernism), or God (Islam). Suffering, they claim, can be eliminated by exerting control over the consequences. We can stop pain by managing physical symptoms, overthrowing the perpetrators, laughing at it, or conforming to strict rules to appease Allah. The only way to deal with evil is to blame others and numb ourselves to its effects.

New spirituality offers a different answer for why we hurt: Since everything that exists is one thing, we experience pain if we're out of sync with universal harmony. The disharmony within us causes our pain.

So what can we do about all the suffering? New spirituality considers suffering an illusion and says that the best response is denial. Just tell yourself it doesn't exist, and it won't. New spirituality borrows heavily from the ancient traditions of Hinduism and Buddhism. Hinduism teaches that the world around us isn't truly real. The secret to freedom from suffering is treating everything as a mere delusion. The Buddhist approach is similar: since attachment is the root cause of suffering, detaching ourselves from desire is the solution.

If the claims of new spirituality are true and suffering is our own fault because we're out of harmony with the universe, where does that leave us? What about babies born with fetal alcohol syndrome or people who suffer all kinds of pain and misery through no fault of their own? How can we say they deserve to suffer?

REFLECT

How do you distinguish between random, undeserved suffering and suffering that could have been avoided if a different path had been chosen? Is there a difference between the effects of the two? Is seemingly undeserved suffering avoidable if a person just has enough foresight and wisdom? How did you arrive at your conclusions?

IDEAS ABOUT THE MEANING AND NATURE OF PAIN

Modern advances in medicine and technology often give us a false sense of control over suffering, and much of life today revolves around preventing or alleviating pain. But pain is as much a philosophical issue as a medical one. Enlightenment-era philosopher René Descartes theorized that pain is a physical sensation, not a spiritual one. At a time when Christianity was under fire for supposedly encouraging people to suffer as Jesus did, this was a welcome improvement. But the truth is that Christians throughout history have taken the lead in *alleviating* human suffering, not promoting it.

A secret battle is raging over what suffering means and what ought to be done about it. New spirituality is gaining the upper hand in this battle with its view that pain is essentially meaningless and the best response is to numb it. That may alleviate physical pain, but if the pain is spiritual in nature, physical remedies won't make us feel better, and they can cause more problems than they solve. The world is filled with spiritual pain, which has led to a heartbreaking increase in suicide, especially among young people.

We all sense that things aren't as they should be—even those who believe that suffering is meaningless and illusory. Faced with so much suffering in the world, we urgently need someone to show us how to vanquish our pain. This battle of ideas must be won, and as we'll see, someone has already provided the solution!

REMEMBER THE FOUR I'S WHEN COMBATING BAD IDEAS ABOUT SUFFERING

1. Identify symptoms of a bad idea.
2. Isolate the bad from the good.
3. Inform others about bad ideas.
4. Invest in those controlled by bad ideas.

HOW JESUS HEALS OUR HURTS

In chapter 6 of *The Secret Battle of Ideas about God* (pages 85–86), we read about World War II veteran Ernest Gordon's experience in the infamous Chungkai prison camp. Two remarkable events transformed this camp, which could be described only as hell on earth. Two prisoners gave their lives for their fellow POWs. One gave away his own food so that his bunkmate would survive; the other confessed to a theft he didn't commit to save his fellow POWs from being executed for the infraction.

Following these sacrificial acts, the attitude in the camp shifted from "me first" to "you first." As the men cared for one another, life gradually regained meaning, and their humanity was restored.

The account of how Gordon and his fellow POWs overcame the horrors of the prison camp offers deep insight into how a Christian worldview can heal us from the idea viruses that threaten to multiply our suffering.

REFLECT

Think of a time the caring help of others alleviated your suffering. It could have been a friend coming alongside you, a mentor sharing wisdom, or someone giving time and attention to help relieve your pain. Why did the presence and involvement of another person help? Do you think that giving and receiving help when it's needed most is the whole story when it comes to suffering?

The Christian worldview doesn't put a smiling face on suffering. The entire book of Job records the story of a godly man who suffered unimaginable loss. Job's children died, his business was destroyed, and a painful skin disease racked his body. Yet even when his wife advised him to curse God and die, Job refused to stop seeking God in his pain (see Job 2:9–10).

A person can replace anger with humility and self-pity with compassion. New spirituality advocates blaming others, numbing the pain, or simply denying that suffering exists. But the Christian worldview offers a much more robust solution to the problem of pain.

Jesus boldly declared, "In the world you will have tribulation. But take heart; I have overcome the world" (John 16:33). The word *overcome* in Koine Greek is *nikao*. *Nikao* doesn't just mean "winning"; it means "outlasting the enemy by depriving him of the power to harm." Jesus confronted suffering on the battlefield and disarmed it! It can no longer rob us of what really matters. Pain and death on this earth will endure until Jesus returns, but the battle has been won. Jesus overcame death, and in him, we are overcomers too.

REFLECT

Read Romans 12:21; 1 John 2:13–14; 4:4; Revelation 2:7; and 21:7. In light of the definition of the Greek word *nikao*, do you understand these verses differently? How does the fact that Jesus has overcome the world change how we view suffering?

I Cor. 15

GAINING NEEDED INSIGHT

The answer to suffering isn't an idea but a person. Four insights from the Bible set the stage for God's magnificent redemptive work:

1. **God knows everything and can do as he chooses.** God knows everything that can possibly be known in the entire universe. He is the perfect source of all knowledge and truth. Because God is all-knowing, he is in charge of the past, present, and future, and he will accomplish his purposes for the world.

2. **God does not choose to *do* everything.** God can do whatever he chooses, but he doesn't always choose to do everything. Islam teaches that because God controls everything, free will is an illusion. In contrast, the Bible teaches that we aren't puppets. God gave us free choice to act meaningfully within the world of laws he created.

3. **Humans choose to sin.** God didn't create us to mechanically say "I love you" like a stuffed animal with a microchip recording. He created us with free choice and the potential for evil, and humans have chosen to act on that potential, causing one another great pain. Authentic love means choosing love even though we're free to choose sin and hate.

4. **God chooses to redeem.** When Jesus died on the cross, he disarmed sin and the suffering it brings so they can no longer destroy us. Like the apostle

Peter, who denied Jesus but was later forgiven and restored, we can find redemption in Christ. No matter where our choices lead us, God knows our destination, and he'll meet us there.

The life of Jesus offered up in our place is God's answer to suffering. The cross gives us hope that God will conquer evil. Human-centered worldviews offer only logical arguments to deal with suffering. The Christian worldview offers a person who suffered, died, and rose again to turn back the effects of sin. Jesus didn't medicate suffering; he overcame it.

Idea viruses seek to convince us that suffering is pointless and devoid of meaning. But knowing that God is with us in our suffering changes the whole story arc. Jesus is the answer to the dilemma of evil and suffering in this world. He is our hope in suffering, and because of him, our pain has meaning.

REFLECT

Much of our suffering results from choices we make when we fail to heed the teachings of God. Our decisions, ideas, and actions have consequences, and we will encounter those consequences. Reflect on our tendency to disobey God and suffer the consequences.

HOW WE ARE THE ANSWER

Historically, Christians embraced and lived out Jesus's teachings about loving our neighbors (see Mark 12:31) and caring for the sick (see Matt. 25:34–40). When disasters and epidemics like the Roman plagues and the Black Death in Europe caused people, including doctors, to flee in fear, Christians risked their lives to care for the afflicted. They were convinced that Jesus would care for their souls in the afterlife just as he instructed them to care for bodily needs (see John 14:1–3). Christians didn't just seek to alleviate pain; they also ministered to deeper needs.

God is personally involved in turning back suffering, and we get to help in his redemptive work on a practical level. A Christian worldview of suffering leads to action. In chapter 6 of *The Secret Battle of Ideas about God* (pages 95–96), I mention five ways we can live out a Christ-centered worldview:

1. **Dwell on God's presence.** God is here with us right now, even if we aren't aware of him. Ask God to help you sense his presence in your everyday life. Constantly remembering that he is with us in our suffering puts it in perspective.

2. **Serve.** Galatians 6:2 says, "Bear one another's burdens." We often find relief for our own suffering when we help others in need. Make a habit of serving others.

3. **Reject fate.** Instead of giving up when change seems impossible or hopeless, we need to follow

the example of Christians like Amy Carmichael. One of the first to stand against sex trafficking, she modeled Christ's love with a warm heart and changed thousands of lives.

4. **Accept the love of others.** When my marriage broke up and I called out for help, people responded. The body of Christ functions best when we faithfully play our parts and serve one another. If someone offers help, accept it. If someone needs help, give it.

5. **Look forward to a better day.** Death is a constant, not a variable. The variable is how we live each day God gives us. That's why the psalmist wrote, "Teach us to number our days that we may get a heart of wisdom" (Ps. 90:12). Wisdom reminds us that a better life awaits us, when sin and suffering will come to an end.

The cross is the centerpiece of human history. Jesus has overcome sin, suffering, and death forever! Because he is the victor (see 1 Cor. 15:55–57), we can confidently reject the idea viruses that promise false answers to suffering.

REFLECT

Read John 16:33 and Romans 8:35–39. Jesus's power and his victory over brokenness mean that we have real hope of healing and redemption. Do you find that having faith in Christ elevates you above the suffering you experience? If not, what is there that surpasses this as a solution? Consider what happens if you're wrong.

DOES MY LIFE HAVE MEANING?

How Idea Viruses Strip Us of Direction and Leave Us Aimless

DISCUSSING CHAPTERS 7 AND 8 OF
THE SECRET BATTLE OF IDEAS ABOUT GOD

You did not choose me, but I chose you and appointed you.

John 15:16

What got you out of bed this morning? On a day-to-day basis, what energizes you? When you consider your life as a whole, what gives it purpose and meaning?

Talk of long-term goals, vision, legacy, making our lives count, giving back to the community all boils down to one question: Why are we here? In other words, what is our reason for being?

Without clear goals we would lack direction, but we often settle for achieving goals without understanding how this fits into the bigger picture. We focus on strategies for making improvements and plotting the best ways to achieve more. But what about the intangible truth that gives meaning to our lives and guides us?

When we understand the meaning of the big story, it sheds light on all of life. The activities of life—today's deadlines, an overcrowded schedule, and rushing to get everything done—tend to distract us. But are we allowing the daily clutter to keep us from grasping the big story that gives shape and meaning to our time on earth?

According to John Stonestreet, postmodernism has saturated our world. This counterfeit worldview denies that one overarching story makes sense of life and gives order to the universe. Instead, postmodernism insists that each of us has a story and all these little stories are of equal importance and validity. However, little stories do nothing to clarify our search for purpose and meaning in life.

If every story is equally valid, then one person's story of hate and violence can claim moral equality with a story of generosity, compassion, and service. As John Stonestreet points out, the postmodern mind-set has led to the unquestioning acceptance of moral relativism. But if nothing is fixed or absolute, what determines the meaning of our lives? Does each person create his or her own meaning, and what if your meaning is in direct opposition to mine?

Where does placing undue value on the small stories lead us? To a purposeless existence, as evidenced by many young people today. A sense of purposelessness, however, runs counter to our innermost being. We have been made for meaning.

REFLECT

Have the little stories coming from social media, entertainment, news, and other sources ever caused you to feel overwhelmed? What effect did this have on you? Does the distraction of small stories deter you from seeking clarity on the ultimate meaning and purpose of your life? If so, how?

Each of us is swept up in a search for meaning—it's part of being human. But the search also makes us vulnerable to idea viruses spread by those who promise they have the answer to the meaning of life. This opens a major new front in the secret battle of ideas.

In chapter 7 of *The Secret Battle of Ideas about God* (pages 99–101), we read about the life of Friedrich Nietzsche, nicknamed the Little Pastor. Nietzsche started out with a deeply held commitment to Christ, but he eventually reached the conclusion that "gods" were just human creations and Jesus was nothing more than a good role model. God was dead, and Christianity's influence had come to an end. With all the extraordinary scientific and economic advancements taking place, humans no longer needed God.

If God is dead, as Nietzsche believed, where are we to find answers to the questions we as humans can't escape? "Does my life count for anything?" "Are my hopes and dreams pointless?" "Does my existence on this planet matter?" Belief in God was once the guiding hand of

Western civilization in the areas of morality and meaning. Now that God is supposedly dead, who or what will take his place? Nietzsche thought that "superhumans" would fill that role. This idea led to unthinkable consequences through Adolf Hitler and his killing machine.

By the middle of the twentieth century, people needed to know more than ever that their lives had meaning and what that meaning was. But where would the search for meaning lead?

REFLECT

When you speak of the meaning of life, what do you mean? Can life have multiple meanings, some more important and some less so? Who is to say what the ultimate meaning of life is?

A POSTMODERN WORLDVIEW: PERSONAL EXPERIENCE DETERMINES MEANING

Without a strong sense of purpose and meaning, people become vulnerable to dangerous ideas. The idea virus of Nazism targeted people who felt oppressed at the hands of unseen enemies. Aimlessness opened a crack into which one of history's worst idea viruses inserted itself.

The five counterfeit worldviews tell us our lives will have meaning if we become part of their sweeping agendas. But most people want everyday meaning that enables them to experience love in their relationships and find joy in their work.

In the small stories of our lives, idea viruses hitch a ride in the myriad messages that bombard us, and we're left with fragmented plot points but no overarching narrative to hold them together. It's easy to conclude there is no master narrative, no fixed standard for truth that puts everything else in perspective. Personal experience is our only source of meaning. That's the essential claim of the postmodern worldview.

It's alarming that postmodernism has embraced the same ideas of Nietzsche that gave rise to the Nazis and their horrific acts of brutality, unfettered by any moral code. An idea virus that started with the writings of a philosopher turned madman in his twisted search for meaning spread into a pandemic that poisoned Europe and the world.

Postmodernists insist that life has no meaning or overarching truth and we ought to be suspicious of anyone who claims it does. They often say things like "I define myself" or "It may be true for you but not for me." But measuring yourself by yourself is like pretending you are magnetic north and attempting to navigate through uncharted wilderness without a compass. Not only would you be forever lost, but you'd also mislead everyone who looked to you for guidance.

To the postmodern worldview, nothing is to be gained by searching "out there" for meaning when we are our own authority and personal experience is our only source of meaning. Ultimately, meaning is an illusion, like peeling layer after layer of an onion until nothing remains.

If each of us had a strong sense of purpose, we might be able to resist idea viruses like postmodernism. But where can we find reliable answers to our questions about meaning? Is there, in fact, a higher purpose that can make our lives meaningful? I believe there is.

REFLECT

Have you ever relied on your own experience as your guide, even when recognized experts and other authorities gave different advice? Are you convinced that your experiences serve as a more accurate and reliable guide to finding life's meaning? If so, how did you arrive at that conclusion?

A CHRISTIAN WORLDVIEW OF MEANING

When philosophers ponder the concept of meaning, they seek answers to three questions:

- What is real?
- How can we know?
- How should we live?

According to Stanford University professor William Damon, only one in five Americans ages twelve to twenty-two say they know where they want to go in life, what they want to accomplish, and why.[2] This is a generation without a destination.

Most people sense that life is something more than the ordinary existence they experience on a daily basis. Each worldview must account for this sense that there has to be more. But some counterfeit worldviews hold that a search for meaning is useless because the only meaning is that which we make for ourselves.

The Christian worldview stands apart from counterfeit worldviews that insist a search for meaning is useless because we create meaning for ourselves. At the intersection of confusion and death, Jesus pointed in a new direction, declaring that our lives can have meaning. "The thief comes only to steal and kill and destroy," he said. "I came that they may have life and have it abundantly" (John 10:10). Abundant life is no fantasy.

In the search for meaning, many wander aimlessly in a shroud of fog without even realizing they're lost. Others, who encounter dense fog, give up the search. Still others, braving the fog, lose their bearings and panic. Only a few navigate successfully toward clarity. The Bible explains why: they hear a voice calling them and follow that voice through confusion, past obstacles, beyond doubt, and into meaning.

The Christian worldview says we find meaning when we listen to the voice of Christ and follow him. Jesus has all authority (see Matt. 28:18), and everything in the universe belongs to him. Seeing Christ in this way opens our hearts and souls to his call.

REFLECT

Abraham Kuyper said, "There is not one square inch of the entire creation about which Jesus Christ does not cry out, 'This is mine! This belongs to me!'"[3] Read Matthew 28:18. How does this view of Jesus's authority change how we live and view God's calling? What can we do this week to give recognition to his authority over our lives?

As God's unique creation, we are made for great things. Psalm 139:13–14 says, "You [God] formed my inward parts; you knitted me together in my mother's womb. I praise you, for I am fearfully and wonderfully made." God designed us to be like him, to bear his image, the *imago Dei*. Unlike the kings in Bible times who erected statues of themselves to display their glory and authority, God formed living, breathing humans to display his glory.

As his image bearers, we reflect God's glory and purposes. The Bible refers to this as a calling. Romans 8:28 says, "We know that for those who love God all things work together for good, for those who are called according to his purpose." The word *call* is related to the Greek word *kaleo*. It means "to summon." Our Creator and Redeemer summons us. Sometimes *kaleo* is translated "vocation." Though we often think of a vocation as a job, it's so much more than that. A calling or vocation gives meaning to our lives.

When we pursue God's purposes, we reflect his glory more brightly. But when we go our own way, we exchange that glory for a counterfeit, like settling for cheap Mardi Gras beads instead of the brilliant splendor of the Hope Diamond (see Jer. 2:11).

When we allow idea viruses to overwhelm us, we end up looking to ourselves for meaning in life. The Christian worldview restores meaning to our lives, pointing us to our Creator and Redeemer, who summons each of us to reflect his glory.

REFLECT

Read Luke 14:15–24, which tells Jesus's parable of calling people to a wedding feast. The honored guests refused to come, distracted by other responsibilities. They missed the one thing that would have given meaning to the rest of their lives. They couldn't—or wouldn't—hear the call. How can we avoid making the same mistake?

HOW JESUS'S CALL FREES US FROM IDEA VIRUSES

God made work and gave it value. He called Adam to work in the garden of Eden and watch over it (see Gen. 2:15). Interestingly, the Hebrew word for work, *abad*, means both "to serve" and "to worship."[4] Work is worship, and worship is work. So Adam apparently experienced work as worship that drew him closer to God.

After the fall, work became drudgery. God cursed the ground because of Adam's sin, and ever since, work has involved pain and toil (see Gen. 3:17). Sin corrupted work and caused us to lose our way. God has shown us the path that leads to life, but most have chosen the way of death. That's the human predicament: we have lost our way.

The purpose we lost in the fall is regained through Christ, who redeemed us on a wooden cross and fashioned for us a holy calling of purpose and grace (see 2 Tim. 1:9). This calling restores meaning in three ways:

1. Calling secures our identities.
2. Calling wards off idea viruses.
3. Calling makes every area of our lives meaningful.

REFLECT

Do you agree that calling transforms the drudgery of work and everyday life? Can life still be drudgery even in one's calling?

WHAT DOES THIS MEAN TO YOU?

God is calling to each of us, but are we listening? The Christian worldview alone shows us four steps we can take to hear God's call and find meaning in life:

1. **Tune in to God's revelation in creation.** Beauty reminds us that we aren't the center of the universe. Like David, we find ourselves humbled when we see the awesome beauty of creation. The created world calls us to surrender to God's voice (see Ps. 8:3–4). Make a point of looking for beauty in the natural world every day and giving praise to God.

2. **Start discovering your unique design.** No two people are alike. God created each of us with unique gifts and motivated abilities. You can discover yours by asking these questions: What activities energize me and make me feel more alive? What do I long for? What captivates my imagination?

3. **Rethink the value of work.** God wants us to find meaning in our work. Meaning grows as we build on our experiences. Like Maestro Maazel, who told my brother the secret to becoming a great conductor (see page 122 of the book), if we want to become more accomplished at something, we must work at improving our skills *every day* for the rest of our lives. Daily improvement is the route to success.

4. Find activities that create flow. Flow weaves together our unique design and the value of work. We find flow and meaning when we work hard at discovering that which deeply compels us. We know we've discovered flow when we're so engrossed in a fulfilling task that we forget about ourselves and lose track of time. Focus your energy and attention on identifying the kinds of activities that create flow and meaning in your life.

It's through calling that God shows us the way to meaning. In your search for meaning, listen for the voice of God, not the counterfeit voices vying for your attention. When he calls you, get moving. He will lead you to discover what you were made for. That, and nothing else, will define the meaning of your life.

REMEMBER THE FOUR I'S WHEN COMBATING BAD IDEAS ABOUT MEANING

1. Identify symptoms of a bad idea.

2. Isolate the bad from the good.

3. Inform others about bad ideas.

4. Invest in those controlled by bad ideas.

7-28-19

Gal 5:26

WHY CAN'T WE JUST GET ALONG?

How Idea Viruses Destroy the Peace We Crave

DISCUSSING CHAPTERS 9 AND 10 OF
THE SECRET BATTLE OF IDEAS ABOUT GOD

✸ *If possible, so far as it depends on you, live peaceably with all.*

Romans 12:18

We all know the tension that develops between two people having a disagreement. Accusations are leveled, and things are said that should have been left unsaid. A conflict that should have been resolved is left to simmer. Each person feels wronged and places blame on the other. A valued relationship has been broken.

Conflict affects us most deeply when it damages personal relationships, but it is no less disruptive in other areas of life. An endless array of issues can drive a wedge between people, such as religious and ideological differences, disputes with neighbors, generational differences, unfair treatment, and false assumptions.

The destructive effects of conflict are seen on a national and global scale as well. Refugees flee war-torn countries. Families are torn apart in civil wars. And people live with the constant, low-level fear of terrorism and nuclear war.

None of us wants to live this way, but where can we find the solution to conflict?

Some idea viruses insist that conflict is someone else's fault. To find the source of conflict, we must look outward, not inward. The Marxist worldview is a leading example of this idea virus. Marxists view the wealthy as the source of all conflict. Wealth, they assert, is a fixed commodity, which means that when one person gains assets, someone else necessarily loses. Limited resources inevitably pit the rich against the poor. Since we all need money to pay for the necessities of life, this wealth inequality leads to conflict.

According to the Marxist worldview, the solution to inequality and conflict is revolution. World peace is attained not by helping the poor but through revenge.

In the West, the strategy for achieving wealth equality is far more insidious than advocating the violent overthrow of the rich. This idea virus whispers lies that we're predisposed to believe. Who wouldn't believe that the wealthy are causing our difficulties and must have broken the rules to get ahead in life?

But history has shown the glaring failures of Marxist theory in resolving the problem of conflict. Only the Christian worldview has the solution for broken relationships and communities. The key is found in the Old Testament concept of *shalom*, a word rich in meaning that refers to peace and wholeness. When shalom instead of revenge guides our approach to resolving conflict, the outcome is peace of mind as well as healthy, restored relationships. Rather than seeking someone else to blame, we look inward to identify the source of conflict.

In this session, we'll explore the lies of Marxism and seek to understand and practice shalom.

REFLECT

When your life is interrupted by relational conflict, what is your natural instinct? For instance, do you find reasons to blame the other person and explain away your own role in the matter? Do you find it difficult to look at yourself objectively and point to words, actions, attitudes, and assumptions that contributed to a broken relationship? Try to be specific, thinking of a recent conflict that affected you.

CONFLICT AND ITS DESTRUCTIVE WORK

The fallout from conflict is seen not only in the lives of friends and family members but also on a much larger scale. In chapter 9 of *The Secret Battle of Ideas about God* (pages 127–28), I describe the far-reaching consequences of a car-bomb attack in Pakistan that killed the founder of Al-Qaeda and two of his sons. This bomb blast ignited a secret battle over worldviews on a global scale. With the rise of Osama bin Laden, Al-Qaeda's new leader, a deadly new virus slipped noiselessly into humanity's bloodstream.

Al-Qaeda declared war on the West but didn't limit itself to bombs and guns. It also attacked with ideas, recruiting disillusioned Westerners to fight for the cause. Today many ISIS fighters come from Europe and the United States.

Bloodshed, terrorism, and war produce a constant hum of uncertainty and fear, ensuring that peace remains elusive. Unfortunately, this is the story of nearly all of human history.

In this battle of ideas, we're not only at war with others; we're also at war with ourselves. Conflict ultimately gives rise to death. "Death and life are in the power of the tongue," says Proverbs 18:21. With every harsh word we speak, we bring death to relationships— and die a little ourselves.

We need to examine the false idea that someone else is responsible for the conflict that affects us. As we do, we need to understand what this idea virus tells us to do about conflict. We can no longer afford to remain unaware of the lie. In seeking a solution, let's begin by locating the source of conflict.

REFLECT

When you talk about conflict, what do you mean? Do you think of conflict as something that takes place mostly on an interpersonal, relational level? Or do you feel that conflict causes the greatest impact and damage on a large scale through violent crime, terrorism, and war?

CONFLICT IS "OUT THERE," BUT IT'S ALSO "IN HERE"

When Adolf Hitler and Joseph Stalin spread their idea viruses of racial purity and Communism, why did millions of people remain silent and uninvolved as millions of others were being slaughtered?

Nazi and Communist leaders got away with mass murder because citizens tacitly agreed with the underlying ideas these dictatorial regimes aggressively promoted. The people of Germany and Russia didn't see until it was too late where the ideas that initially appealed to them would lead.

Nazi Germany presents an eye-opening history lesson on conflict. Conflict arises when we view ourselves in ways that diminish the value of others. The underlying problem of conflict is as much "in here" as it is "out there." Hitler convinced the German people that the Aryan race was superior and non-Aryans were the enemy. It's a short step from feeling superior to believing the world would be better off without certain kinds of people. A spirit of self-righteousness precedes every act of great evil.

Theories abound regarding the origin of conflict and how to solve it. Many economists view scarcity and competition for finite resources as the real source of conflict. Others claim the culprit is affluenza (having too much), which causes people to act in irresponsible and destructive ways. Idea viruses seek to convince us that the blame always lies out there somewhere and the solution does as well.

Like eighteenth-century philosopher Jeremy Bentham, many people today believe the solution to conflict lies in maximizing happiness and minimizing pain for the greatest number of people. And an increasing number of people consider this the government's job.

But a government big enough to give us everything we want is big enough to take everything we have. History's worst mass murderers—including Stalin, Hitler, and Mao Tse-tung—moved easily from restructuring the government to killing those who stood in their way. An effective method for eliminating the opposition, perhaps, but not the path to peace!

REMEMBER THE FOUR I'S WHEN COMBATING BAD IDEAS ABOUT CONFLICT

1. Identify symptoms of a bad idea.
2. Isolate the bad from the good.
3. Inform others about bad ideas.
4. Invest in those controlled by bad ideas.

PEACE ON EARTH, OR ELSE: THE MARXIST WORLDVIEW

Marxism asserts that society is like an Easter egg hunt, where a few people get all the eggs and the rest end up empty handed. The wealthy have amassed riches by breaking the rules and stealing from the rest of us. We should take back this ill-gotten gain, Marxists say. By force, if necessary. Peace will be possible only when capitalism is destroyed.

The Marxist worldview teaches that short-term pain will lead to long-term gain. In chapter 9 of *The Secret Battle of Ideas about God* (page 138–39), I talk about Che Guevara, the revolutionary who was Fidel Castro's right-hand man in the Cuban Revolution. Che believed that the ends justify the means, but his idealistic vision of

helping the poor transformed into outright brutality and contributed to the dictatorship of Fidel Castro.

Other examples of the deadly consequences of the Marxist idea
virus include the Soviet Union, where tens of thousands succumbed
to executions, genocide, and famine, and Communist China, where
millions died from starvation, hard labor, and beatings.

History shows that the horror extended far beyond China, Cuba,
and Russia. Millions more have perished in countries like Cambodia,
North Korea, and Yugoslavia, where the idea virus of Marxism has
flourished.

REFLECT

No one is fully protected from conflict. Powers at work in the world
so upset the social order that everyone in a region or even a nation is
affected. What do you think motivates leaders and movements that suc-
ceed only by pitting groups of people against one another?

A CHRISTIAN WORLDVIEW OF CONFLICT

After a century of Marxist experimentation, we are further than
ever from an answer to the question "Why can't we just get along?"

It's time to see whether the Christian worldview offers the break-through we seek.

In chapter 10 of *The Secret Battle of Ideas about God* (pages 143–44), we read about Chaplain Henry Gerecke, who worked in a military prison after the Second World War ended. At the prison, Gerecke prayed with Hitler's former deputy führer, Rudolf Hess, and other Nazi war criminals and shared the good news of the gospel with them. The gospel, Gerecke knew, is the secret to restoring the good when everything has gone bad.

As we discussed earlier, the Christian worldview approaches conflict through shalom, which describes what life together looks like in a world God has redeemed. Instead of placing the blame for conflict on others, shalom restores peace, tranquility, and well-being in three ways:

Hebrew in shalom - peace

1. **Shalom acknowledges the conflict *inside* us as well as *among* us.** Evil "in here" and "out there" must be opposed, but shalom promotes unity rather than division because it recognizes that every person bears God's image and has an eternal soul.

2. **Shalom focuses on *giving* rather than *taking*.** Shalom can be received only as we extend it to others. Just as God instructed the exiled Jews living in Babylon to seek shalom for their captors so they might experience it themselves (see Jer. 29:7), we're called to bless our enemies rather than curse them (see Rom. 12:14).

3. Shalom focuses on *love*, not *hate*. Jesus said, "Love your enemies and pray for those who persecute you" (Matt. 5:44). This is shalom in action: responding with grace yet not compromising truth.

Read Romans 12:14–21. The Bible shows that the only solution to conflict is shalom and that shalom overcomes conflict only when we give rather than take. We need to recognize the forces inside us that give rise to conflict, concentrating on love instead of hate. Further, to avoid conflict, we should give up the ingrained habit of seeing people as "them" who are different from and somehow opposed to "us." How can we achieve a shalom lifestyle in our day-to-day lives?

II Tim. 2: 24-25

SHALOM CAN BE RESTORED

Idea viruses have threatened and violated shalom in our world. Counterfeit worldviews insist that shalom is the remnant of a world that has ceased to exist and that peace can be restored only through a revolutionary remaking of society. But this isn't the end of the story.

The Christian worldview says that Christ's sacrifice doesn't just bandage things up so we can limp through life. It restores fullness and wholeness to life, both now and forever. Shalom doesn't wait for the other person to take the first step toward resolving conflict. Change starts with each of us.

Shalom transcends conflict with a positive picture of what peace looks like and how to achieve it in the following three areas:

1. **Shalom restores community.** God relates to us—his image bearers—personally. His life reaches to our lives. He's not a distant deity who broadcasts the laws we must obey from a faraway location. We experience shalom as we live in true community with one another.

2. **Shalom restores creation.** Shalom is a vision for restoration that makes everything better than new. Our very bodies were created for shalom.

3. **Shalom restores communication.** When we dialogue, we communicate the way God communicates (see John 1:1). Dialogue helps people understand one another and focuses on arriving at a good outcome. It builds others up rather than ourselves. Asking "Is this conversation building shalom?" brings clarity and focus to our interactions. Shalom helps us look out for one another, seek one another's best interests, and become friends (see Phil. 2:4).

REFLECT

Do you know someone who needs to lead more of a shalom lifestyle? How can you share shalom? Develop an approach using the Four I's.

WHAT THIS MEANS FOR US

Shalom is the Christian worldview's answer to the pressing question "Why can't we just get along?" We are to "live peaceably with all" (Rom. 12:18) and "not become conceited, provoking one another, envying one another" (Gal. 5:26). But what should we do differently from before? The following four steps show us how to build shalom and defuse conflict:

1. **Replace anger with patience.** Shalom teaches us to "be quick to hear, slow to speak, slow to anger" (James 1:19). Instead of reacting in anger, we learn to patiently wait for the Holy Spirit to adjust our attitudes toward others.

2. **See God's image in others.** It's easy to diminish people we're in conflict with. But the way of shalom tells us that "love is patient and kind"

(1 Cor. 13:4). God sees his children as reflections of his image, and so should we.

3. **Be a peacemaker, not just a peacekeeper.** Shalom isn't just about avoiding conflict; it's also about actively seeking peace in relationships. Being peacemakers often requires offering words of peace to those we find unapproachable.

4. **Never lose hope.** Jesus prayed that his disciples would experience oneness so that the world would see the Father's love and know that he sent Jesus (see John 17:20–23). Following the way of Jesus changes us, enabling us to love and find common ground with those who view life differently from the way we do. That's the power and hope of shalom!

REFLECT

Do the four steps to building shalom seem valid to you? Or does it seem as if they create Christians who are pushovers while rewarding those who stir up strife?

Our well-being as image bearers of God is tied to the well-being of others. This is why shalom pursues peace rather than simply avoiding conflict.

Jesus took the first step toward restoring shalom when he died on the cross, putting an end to the enmity between God and humanity. He is the key to shalom. Love isn't just an idea; it's a life given in our place. In the work Jesus completed on the cross, we find hope that a power greater than our own can transform the things that divide us into the profound unity we all seek.

REFLECT

Reflect on Jesus's death and resurrection to save the world. Do you agree that his death and resurrection are the key to shalom? Do you believe that shalom is the only valid and effective path to overcoming conflict?

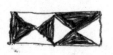

SESSION 6

IS THERE ANY HOPE FOR THE WORLD?

How Idea Viruses Drive Us to Despair

DISCUSSING CHAPTERS 11 AND 12 OF
THE SECRET BATTLE OF IDEAS ABOUT GOD

*I have said these things to you, that in me you may
have peace. In the world you will have tribulation.
But take heart; I have overcome the world.*

John 16:33

The idea virus of despair has afflicted the human race, and it's still
spreading unabated. For millennia, humans have been asking, "Is
there any hope for the world?" And we're still waiting for an answer.

By the end of the nineteenth century, the Western world discovered that civilization was *not* bound by fate, and as a direct
result of that idea, humans achieved greater advances in a century
than during the previous five thousand years. But as we've seen,
ideas have consequences, and with the presumed inevitability of

progress, people embraced a utopian mind-set. God no longer seemed necessary.

But confidence and human initiative fell far short of assuring hope. Fourteen years after the dawn of the twentieth century, humanity received a shocking wake-up call. World War I and the Bolshevik revolution in Russia claimed millions of lives and inflicted unimaginable suffering around the globe. The dawning of a hopeful new era gave way to the bloodiest century in history. And that was twenty years before the outbreak of World War II, when millions more lost their lives! It's hard to conceive of death on the scale witnessed in the twentieth century.

Scientific and technological advances intended to alleviate suffering also led to developing more "efficient" weapons for waging war, which have caused unprecedented violence and suffering. In light of history, it would appear that casting off the deterministic superstition of fate did little to help the world or offer hope to its inhabitants.

Although it's true that science can be directed toward developing more effective delivery systems for death, so can religion. Radical Muslims, for example, have weaponized jihad not because they're poor and uneducated, as many Westerners assume, but because of their religious convictions. Religious zeal, which motivates a hatred of the West and its decadent ways, is the primary motivation behind radical Islamic terrorism. The most committed followers of Allah are ready to sacrifice everything to advance their goal of creating a global Islamic state under the rule of religious leaders and Sharia law.

The threat is real and ongoing, but Jesus is our hope both in this life and in eternity. No matter what might happen, hope endures.

But in the meantime, what are we to do on a day-to-day basis in light of the constant threat of attack? If hatred and violence continue to be the dark preoccupation of humanity, what does it even mean to be human?

The opposite of hope is despair. This side of eternity, we have to learn how to live in the midst of life's uncertainty, hatred, and violence. Conditions are ripe for the spread of idea viruses during times of upheaval, major change, or fundamental shifts in the status quo. When people are searching for explanations and solutions, counterfeit worldviews rush in to provide answers. Islam is the counterfeit worldview we'll examine in this session, and like other idea viruses, Islam presents its own solution to despair, even as it inspires much of what keeps our world unsettled.

REFLECT

Proverbs 13:12 says, "Hope deferred makes the heart sick." At some point, people will stop hoping for something to deliver them from the blackness of despair. When that happens, what will keep them going? Do any of the worldviews we're looking at offer hope for us personally and for civilization as a whole?

HOPE AND THE WORLDVIEW OF ISLAM

In chapter 11 of *The Secret Battle of Ideas about God* (pages 166–68), I note that according to Muslim scholars, radical Islamists lash out at the Western world because they believe the West is a threat to the only thing they think will bring hope: unquestioning obedience to Allah.

The Islamic worldview begins with Muhammad's teaching that all humans are born Muslim, in a state of submission to God, or Allah. But we have been led astray to worship false gods or deny Allah altogether. Mercifully, Allah sent Muhammad and other prophets to speak to the nations and correct these errors of belief and practice (see Quran 16:36; 35:24).

According to Muhammad and the Quran, we are not Allah's image bearers; we are his slaves, and we can know Allah only through obedience to his law, which is our sole responsibility.

When people cease their rebellion against Allah, which happens through jihad, hope will arise. Radical Islamists view this sustained battle against anything that hinders the advance of Islam not as an act of aggression but as a way of offering Allah's mercy to the rebellious. Islamic regimes justify aggressive persecution of nonbelievers, especially Christians, as a means of restoring hope for all who willingly submit to Allah.

Radical Muslims use force in their pursuit of obedience to Allah. Thus far, the military superpowers of the West have no answer to increasing terrorist attacks. Their seeming impotence signals that it's futile to rely on strength to achieve or restore hope. What, then, is the path to hope?

REFLECT

What do you see as the primary contrast between the Christian understanding of humanity's relationship with God and the Islamic teaching of submission and obedience to Allah? Which belief system is more conducive to the type of hope that humanity seeks, and why?

Christians - relationship of love - God
Islam - relationship of fear

IDEA VIRUSES ATTACK, BUT HOPE WINS

In chapter 12 of *The Secret Battle of Ideas about God* (pages 171–72), I tell the story of journalist Mindy Belz, who returned to Mosul, Iraq, five years after her previous visit. She was horrified at how much the city had deteriorated in that time.

The withdrawal of US troops had left a power vacuum that a ruthless warlord named Abu Bakr al-Baghdadi had stepped in to fill. Al-Baghdadi believed that enslaving, killing, and raping Christians pleased Allah. His band of thugs, which Westerners call ISIS, quickly swelled to an army of thousands.

As cities were being destroyed and millions of Christians and other minorities were being driven out or killed, Mindy served as the world's link to a humanitarian crisis of enormous proportions. Yet in the midst of all this death and destruction, believers were sharing their meager provisions and caring for the disabled and wounded at a time when they could barely care for themselves.

Where is hope in a world that seems so dark? Mindy's reporting from Iraq helps us grasp how hope secures victory in the secret battle of ideas, leading to a reliance on the only true hope for the world.

REFLECT

Think about Mindy's travels in war-torn Iraq. It's easy to see the hope-lessness of the situation in Mosul, but what do you see that gives reason for hope? Also consider what God might be doing behind the scenes in the lives of Iraqis and those who go there to render assistance. What would you say is the whole story regarding evidence of hope in a land of war?

WHERE IS THE EVIDENCE OF HOPE?

Every worldview has a story about what evil is, where it came from, and what hope we have of vanquishing it. From a Christian worldview, hope is real and within our grasp.

From God's perspective, hope is the expectation that a better day will come. Hope runs on a parallel track with faith. "Faith is the confidence that what we hope for will actually happen," says the author of Hebrews (11:1 NLT).

The five counterfeit worldviews we've been examining insist that nothing will change unless everything changes: enlightenment will come *only* when religion is abolished; poverty will be eradicated *only* through a worldwide revolution; utopia will be realized *only* when the global population achieves a higher consciousness through meditation.

These worldviews see only the thinnest of possibilities that hope will be realized. Not so with the Christian worldview, and for three surprising reasons:

> **1. Hope helps us live fearlessly.** Fear plays a central role in how most people live and view the future. In chapter 12 of *The Secret Battle of Ideas about God* (pages 176 and 179), I describe my journey through a season of depression. Fear and indecision caused me to lose hope for the future. I knew the danger of giving in to fear but couldn't seem to avoid it. The Christian worldview tells us that the answer to fear is love (see 1 John 4:18). Fear may be strong, but God's love is stronger (see Isa. 41:10).
>
> **2. Hope helps us live resiliently.** Shocking, terrible things happen in everyday life, but hope enables us to withstand the threats we face. With hope, we become resilient, growing through instability

and thriving in disorder. Resilient people don't allow fear or regret to shackle them. Mistakes don't define us; they refine us. One of the best gifts we can give those we love, and one of the most powerful weapons we can deploy against the Evil One, is to set aside past mistakes as the apostle Paul did and live with endurance (see Phil. 3:13–14). As he said in Romans 5:4, "Endurance produces character, and character produces hope."

3. **Hope helps us live confidently.** Hope makes courage possible, and courage fuels confidence. If there is no God and this life is all there is, we have no choice but to orbit around ourselves. Our mistakes, shortcomings, and negative circumstances form a perverse kind of gravity that fuses us to despair. But if we orbit around the heart of the Father, who has removed our sins from us "as far as the east is from the west" (Ps. 103:12) and gives us "a future and a hope" (Jer. 29:11), we are lifted away from the pull of fear and despair.

Love, healing, purpose, and peace find their fulfillment in hope, and hope releases us from the unrelenting idea virus of despair. With its ethic of love, justice, and freedom, the Christian worldview offers the only path to hope in a world of despair and fear.

Hope is expectant waiting.

6. The Lord is on my side; I will not fear. What can man do to me?

REFLECT

Reflecting on the three ways the Christian worldview assures hope, choose one and compare the Christian teaching on hope with your own beliefs and life experience. Do you put more confidence in the Christian worldview on hope or in your own hard-won experience? In either case, how do you know that what you believe is true?

Ps. 118: 7 The Lord is for me among those who help me; Therefore I shall see my desire on those who hate me.

WHAT HOPE MEANS TO YOU

Hope isn't merely an idea, a belief, or a conviction; it is active confidence in God's truth, which leads to significant changes in the way we approach life. Here are four ways we can actively pursue hope in our daily lives:

1. **Face reality head on.** Hope refuses to ignore reality instead of taking refuge in denial or hiding from the truth. Biblical hope isn't wishful thinking, fantasizing, or dreaming of something better in the future; it's a confident assurance that drives back the darkness in this

world. No matter what reality throws at you, embrace hope and approach life squarely and unflinchingly.

2. **Bring work gloves.** In chapter 12 of *The Secret Battle of Ideas about God* (page 181), I mention that after languishing for decades in crime and poverty, my home city of Detroit, Michigan, is rising from the ashes through ministries like Grace Centers of Hope. In a world of despair, hope shows up in overalls, ready to get to work. Find ways to join in the action!

3. **Choose to give life.** Like the Christian workers in Iraq and Syria who are bringing life and hope to people who are suffering at the hands of ISIS, look for opportunities to offer life to those around you who are struggling with despair.

4. **Don't put hope in yourself.** Like the disheartened rich young man instructed to give his possessions to the poor (see Mark 10:17–22), we're often guilty of putting our hope in ourselves and our ability to control our lives. The trap is that when we don't feel in control, we assume that no one is in control, not even God. The problem is that we suffer from unbelief. Hope isn't about willing ourselves to believe something that isn't true; it's about trusting that God knows what he's doing. Seeing God for who he really is restores hope.

REFLECT

Read Mark 9:14–29. Think about this father's honest expression of helplessness. He would have done anything to help his son get well. But he rightly sensed that his son's healing depended on God's power. What does this mean to you personally? Do you have any doubts or an alternative view that you feel is valid?

WHY PEOPLE WITH HOPE DON'T FLEE HARDSHIP

In chapter 12 of *The Secret Battle of Ideas about God* (page 183), I relate a conversation between the Chaldean bishop of Aleppo, Antoine Audo, and journalist Mindy Belz. Two-thirds of Syrian Christians had been either killed or driven away from their homes, but the cleric chose to stay with his people who remained. Hope strengthened his resolve to stay despite the risks involved. Like many Christians in the persecuted church, Bishop Audo was determined to cling to his faith even if he lost everything.

The world can be a dark and terrifying place. Slavery, torture, and death are real. Standing for truth and fighting against evil and injustice seem to get us nowhere. But that's only half the story.

Hope is recruiting people who are willing to take action. This includes you!

REMEMBER THE FOUR I'S WHEN COMBATING BAD IDEAS ABOUT HOPE FOR THE WORLD

1. Identify symptoms of a bad idea.

2. Isolate the bad from the good.

3. Inform others about bad ideas.

4. Invest in those controlled by bad ideas.

8-11-19

IS GOD EVEN RELEVANT?

How Jesus Conquers Idea Viruses Once and for All

DISCUSSING CHAPTER 13 OF
THE SECRET BATTLE OF IDEAS ABOUT GOD

What comes into our minds when we think about
God is the most important thing about us.

A. W. Tozer, *The Knowledge of the Holy*

You have made us and drawn us to yourself, and
our heart is unquiet until it rests in you.

Saint Augustine, *The Confessions of Saint Augustine*

The best-known atheists in America spend a surprising amount of
time talking about God. People don't expend vast amounts of energy
arguing about purely fictional characters, such as mermaids and
gnomes. So why the unceasing debate over God among those who
question or deny his existence? A growing number of people wonder
not just if God exists but whether his existence even matters.

This debate about God hasn't died down because we have a deep
sense that reality includes more than we experience with our five senses.

Ecclesiastes states that God "has put eternity into man's heart" (3:11), which explains why we can't escape the question of God.

Another reason we have trouble escaping this question is that he is a personal God and our lives have meaning in relation to him. When our lives are disrupted and we need help, we tend to look to God either in faith and hope or in anger and doubt. We have a sense that he is either at fault for our circumstances or our only hope. In either case, it's difficult to avoid bringing him into the discussion.

REFLECT

Recall a time you were tempted to dismiss God as a factor in your life but were unable to escape the sense that he was there. What kept you from turning your back on him even when you were filled with doubt or held him responsible for your pain?

God is always there!!!!!!!!

In chapter 13 of *The Secret Battle of Ideas about God* (pages 185–86), I talk about concluding in high school that God simply wasn't relevant to my life. I wouldn't have denied believing in God, but in practice, I was an atheist, moving further away from him in my decisions, values, and priorities.

Every worldview offers a way of salvation. But if what we've seen about the Christian worldview is true, the alternatives can't save us in the way we need to be saved. The Christian worldview says that the answer is to be reconciled to God. C. S. Lewis perfectly summarized what I eventually came to embrace: "I believe in Christianity as I believe that the Sun has risen, not only because I see it, but because by it I see everything else."[5]

How we view the Christian faith shapes our view of the world, but how we understand God shapes it even more. Our thinking about God changes when we learn to see him

- as *creator*, through whom the universe came into being (see Gen. 1:1; John 1:1–3);
- as *sustainer* of the world, holding everything together (see Col. 1:17); and
- as *communicator* to the world, not only through creation but also through Christ.

Seeing God in this way leads us to conclude that he is real, the Bible is true, and the Christian worldview makes sense.

REFLECT

Have you engaged in serious discussions about the existence of God? Has your stance changed over time? What do you mean today when you say that you believe (or do not believe) in God?

WHEN EVERYTHING FALLS APART

As an adult, I pursued the Christian worldview with all my heart. (Read the full story on pages 186–89 in *The Secret Battle of Ideas about God*.) But my life turned upside down when my wife sustained a brain injury in a cycling accident and then chose to end our marriage after she recovered.

Initially I drew closer to God in my pain, pouring myself into worship, prayer, and service. But eventually hope faded, and I came very close to walking away from my faith.

Alarmed at my condition, some of my buddies invited me to reboot on a weeklong hunting trip. During the trip, I broke. The only words that came out when I tried to pray were "God, what did I do to deserve this? I have *loved* you. I have *served* you. *What more do you want from me?*"

I argued with God, pleaded with him to relieve my pain, and burst out again in defiant curses. The pain inside alerted me to idea viruses lodged in my heart and mind: I was unloved, I was a failure, and there was no hope.

In the end, my childhood faith in Jesus restored the love, healing, purpose, peace, and hope I craved.

Life tosses us around like a rowboat in gale-force winds. We encounter difficulties because of the way our fallen world operates and, at times, because we experience the consequences of choices we've made. Perhaps you sought love but settled for lust or desired healing but settled for numbness. You might have settled for busyness in an attempt to crowd out a longing for meaning. Or maybe you desired peace but settled for isolation, silence, or detachment.

The gospel is good news not only for those who are learning for the first time that God loves them, that Jesus died for them and rose again, and that God offers them forgiveness and the free gifts of grace and salvation. The gospel is also good news for those who already love Jesus but struggle with what the life of faith looks like in everyday life.

REFLECT

Have you experienced a serious crisis of faith that led you to the brink of rejecting God and seeking a different path in life? What brought about the crisis? How did you process the spiritual conflict you were facing?

TWO WAYS WE EACH NEED TO KNOW GOD

Most believers think reconciliation with God involves simply trusting Jesus as their Savior. But that's only part of the story. If we want to escape the idea viruses that keep us from experiencing the good life, we need to understand two things:

1. **Reconciliation is a journey *to* God.** The first
   part of getting right with God is repentance

(*metanoia* in Greek), which means "changing one's way of life." The New Testament says that Jesus is *the* way to God (see John 14:6). He is the Messiah, "God with us" (see Isa. 7:14; Matt. 1:23). The Bible presents humans as criminals whose sin establishes our guilt, but the Judge of the universe offers us complete pardon in Christ (see Rom 5:8). We don't have to be good enough to be reconciled to God. Change comes through Christ's sacrifice, not before it, and leads us straight to God.

2. **Reconciliation is a journey *with* God.** In trusting Jesus, we come to *know* God so we can *love* him. The journey itself, though, is a moment-by-moment relationship with God. We *love* him to truly *know* him. This is what he intended when he reconciled us to himself.

In chapter 13 of *The Secret Battle of Ideas about God* (pages 195–96), I share the story of a young woman named Bek, who found herself struggling with deep despair. After years of trusting God with everything, she gave up, feeling he wasn't there when she needed him most.

At the Summit, Bek regained confidence not only that God is real but that he also loves her and has a plan for her life and the world. As she experienced the staff's unconditional love for her, she opened her heart to God and his healing. Reconciliation led her back to hope and a lifelong journey with God.

HOW TO LIVE AS IF JESUS'S PROMISES ARE TRUE

The five counterfeit worldviews we've been studying promise answers to life's deepest questions but end up multiplying our misery. In stark contrast, if we believe in Jesus, he enables us to embrace the truth of these five promises:

Faith Triumphs in Trouble

1. **I am loved** (see Rom. 5:1–5). Deep, unconditional love exists, and it's yours as a follower of
   Jesus. God's agape love—a selfless, gentle, hopeful, self-giving love—harmonizes all other loves,
   and it never fails. We can offer agape to others
   because God has poured it out into our hearts. A
   homeless man may seem lazy or weak willed to
   me, but agape spotlights his loveliness because of
   Jesus's kind of love.

2. **My suffering will be overcome** (see John
   16:29–33). Jesus conquered the world's troubles
   on the cross, forever depriving evil of its ability
   to harm us. And one day Jesus will wipe away
   every tear (see Rev. 21:4). The peace he offers
   is not of this world (see John 14:27). When we
   reach out to others who are suffering, we can
   walk alongside them without trying to fix them.
   Pain isn't a sign that Jesus has lost the victory; it's
   a reminder that we haven't yet experienced the
   full extent of his triumph.

3. **I have an incredible calling** (see John 15:12–17). Carl Sagan and King David both gazed at the same expanse of heaven, yet Sagan, a God denier, saw his own significance in light of his own smallness. David, a God embracer, saw his own significance in light of God's bigness. Because of God, we aren't lost in the cosmos. Life has meaning when we see it from God's perspective. God has also called us to restored meaning because we bear his image. When work is frustrating, we can be confident we're doing the job for a higher purpose. When relationships are a challenge, we can know without a doubt that we're called to community and can keep investing in one another.

4. **I am meant for community** (see Rom. 12:14–18). The Christian worldview says that *v. 19* sin causes conflict, breaking our relationships with God and others. Healing begins with shalom, a vision of a peacefully content life in which our needs are met as we meet the needs of others. What is broken becomes unbroken. Shalom doesn't just hold things together until we're rescued from this planet; it places us right in the middle of real life, where decayed things need repairing, evil needs opposing,

and ugly things need beautifying. Instead of avoiding conflict, we press into it, seeing other people as image bearers of God.

5. **There is hope for the world** (see **Rom. 12:9–12**). What is right and just and true will win. Hope seems far off for those who embrace idea viruses, because they think nothing will change unless everything changes. From a Christian worldview, however, hope is real. When we're discouraged, we can remember that Jesus died to save the world and then rose from the dead (see 1 Cor. 15:3–4). No power on earth can change that fact. No matter what life throws at us, hope in Jesus gives us confidence.

These five declarations confront the stealth attacks of idea viruses. But as necessary and true as they are, these declarations pale in comparison with the coming reality of Jesus's return to claim his own. Revelation 5:9–13 says that at the end of all things, the redeemed will sing a new song to Jesus, the One who made every good thing possible. "To him who sits on the throne and to the Lamb be blessing and honor and glory and might forever and ever!" (v. 13).

Fear and despair cannot destroy us, because Jesus has already won the battle of ideas. His love is unconditional. His victory is unconquerable. His purpose is unassailable. His peace is unbreakable. His hope is undeniable.

REFLECT

Read the five declarations of freedom and the corresponding Bible passages listed. Ponder each declaration and ask yourself whether it speaks to your spirit as the truth of God. If it does, how will that change the way you think and the way you live? Think back to the previous sessions in this study and ask yourself how you know that the five declarations are true.

IDEA VIRUSES

COUNTERFEIT WORLDVIEW IDEAS

Secularism. The problem is God.

Marxism. The problem is the rich.

Postmodernism. The problem is our obsession with truth.

New spirituality. The problem is that we don't realize we're God.

Islam. The problem is rebellion against Allah.

COUNTERFEIT WORLDVIEW IDEAS ABOUT LOVE

Secularism. We shouldn't guilty about taking what we want; freedom from restraint promises the truest freedom.

Marxism. Capitalists rig the system to cause us to always want more than we have.

Postmodernism. We speak of love only to mask what we're after, which is sex.

New spirituality. The universe is love, and we are part of the universe. Therefore, we are love. If we don't feel loved, it's because we're not familiar enough with our universal power of love.

Islam. If you don't feel loved, it's because you haven't earned it through submission to Allah.

COUNTERFEIT WORLDVIEW IDEAS ABOUT PAIN AND SUFFERING

Secularism. People should stop questioning why pain exists and instead focus on managing the suffering so that we can regain control.

Marxism. We experience pain because the rich have left us in misery by taking more than their fair share.

Postmodernism. There is no sure answer for why we endure pain and suffering. We should embrace the absurd and quit expecting answers to questions that make no sense to begin with.

New spirituality. We must realize that pain is an illusion and the best response is to deny it exists.

Islam. We should stop asking questions about pain and suffering because Allah is in complete control. We must simply obey.

COUNTERFEIT WORLDVIEW IDEAS ABOUT MEANING IN LIFE

Secularism. There is no ultimate meaning—the material world is all there is. Every problem is a material problem and therefore can be addressed only by a material solution.

Marxism. People need to rise up and overcome through revolution against outside forces that keep them from living meaningful lives.

Postmodernism. Only when we realize that life is meaningless will we find true freedom.

New spirituality. Only when we rid ourselves of ego and become one with the universe can we be set free from meaninglessness.

Islam. We can find meaning only through total submission to Allah.

COUNTERFEIT WORLDVIEW IDEAS ABOUT PEACE

Secularism. The problem is that people worry about religion and the supernatural. They should focus instead on the here and now.

Marxism. The problem is that the rich have broken the rules and taken unfairly from the rest of us. Capitalism must be destroyed in order to gain world peace.

Postmodernism. The problem is that people pursue truth, which leads to conflict.

New spirituality. The problem is that we are selfish, egotistical, and not one with the love of the universe.

Islam. The problem is that too many people do not submit to Allah.

COUNTERFEIT WORLDVIEW IDEAS ABOUT HOPE

Secularism. People should live for the here and now. There is no heaven.

Marxism. There is no salvation without the overthrow of the rich.

Postmodernism. There is no ultimate meaning, so hope is up to us to work out individually.

New spirituality. We must embrace our divinity.

Islam. Hope is found in total submission to Allah.

SUMMIT METHOD OF INQUIRY

At Summit Ministries, when discussing topics—especially controversial ones—with people who embrace other worldviews, we employ a method of engagement that relies on honest inquiry. We use this method to give form to the discussion and guide us through the process of clarifying meanings, identifying the origins of ideas, examining the contexts of ideas, assessing truth versus falsehood, and considering the most likely outcomes of adopting false ideas rather than the truth. As we seek to engage people and transform culture, we ask the following questions:

- What do you mean?
- How did you arrive at that conclusion?
- Do you think that's the whole story?
- How do you know that what you believe is true?
- What happens if you're wrong?

When you're discussing the six worldviews with others, ask them these questions. They will not only deepen your understanding of your own worldview, but they will also help you understand the perspectives of others and the ideas they believe.

NOTES

1. C. S. Lewis, *The Problem of Pain* (New York: HarperOne, 2015), 91.

2. William Damon, *The Path to Purpose: How Young People Find Their Calling in Life* (New York: Free Press, 2008), 8.

3. Abraham Kuyper, *Near unto God: Daily Meditations Adapted for Contemporary Christians by James C. Schaap* (Grand Rapids, MI: CRC, 1997), 7.

4. See *abad*, Strong's Hebrew reference number 5647, in Robert L. Thomas, ed., *New American Standard Exhaustive Concordance of the Bible: Hebrew-Aramaic and Greek Dictionaries* (Nashville: Holman, 1981), 1569.

5. C. S. Lewis, *The Weight of Glory : And Other Addresses* (New York: HarperOne, 2001), 140.

DEFEND YOUR FAITH FROM THE DANGEROUS IDEAS OF OTHER WORLDVIEWS

Only 3 percent of Americans currently have a biblical worldview. Are you and your church members among them?

This curriculum kit draws readers into the book *The Secret Battle of Ideas about God* through a seven-session DVD—with Bible teachers including Del Tackett, John Stonestreet, and Sean McDowell—and an accompanying participant's guide. The complete kit is ideal for small-group discussion, Sunday school classes, and churches.

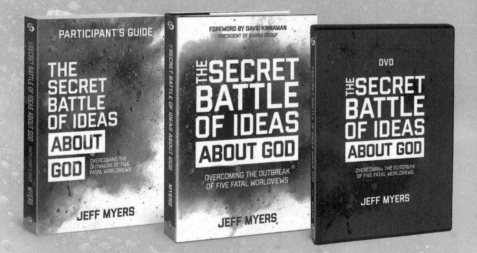

Get a special deal for your church by calling 800.323.7543